APRIL FULTZ

# A Forest of Life Giving Trees

### 31-Day Prayer Guide to Live a Fruitful Life

**A Forest of Life Giving Trees: 31-Day Prayer Guide to Live a Fruitful Life**
Copyright © 2025 April Fultz

Published by Clay Bridges Press in Houston, TX
www.ClayBridgesPress.com

All rights reserved. No part of this publication may be reproduced, stored in a retrieval system, or transmitted in any form by any means, electronic, mechanical, photocopy, recording, or otherwise, without the prior permission of the publisher, except as provided for by USA copyright law.

Unless otherwise indicated, all scripture quotations are are taken from the ESV® Bible (The Holy Bible, English Standard Version®), copyright © 2001 by Crossway, a publishing ministry of Good News Publishers. Used by permission. All rights reserved.

ISBN: 978-1-68488-125-3 (Paperback)
ISBN: 978-1-68488-126-0 (Hardback)
eISBN: 978-1-68488-127-7

Special Sales: Most Clay Bridges titles are available in special quantity discounts. Custom imprinting or excerpting can also be done to fit special needs. Contact Clay Bridges at Info@ClayBridgesPress.com

**To my children and descendants.**

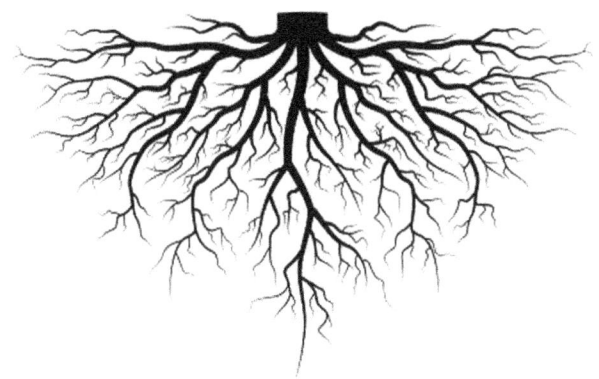

The LORD bless you and keep you;
the Lord make his face to shine upon you and be gracious to you;
the LORD lift up his countenance upon you and give you peace.
Numbers 6:24-26

# Introduction

Susan Hunt wrote a compelling book entitled *The True Woman*; I learned a lot from it, but one truth that stuck with me is the idea of being a life-giver.[1] In Hebrew, Eve means "the mother of all living" (Genesis 3:20). In other words, Eve was responsible for bringing life to all humanity.

Like Eve, as believers, we have a sacred responsibility. In every season and situation, we are called to be life-givers—spiritual life-givers—and bless the world around us. This truth, coupled with living in Virginia, surrounded by trees, inspired me to write this book.

Have you ever walked through a forest? Imagine it—the smell of pine, the soft leaves, and the soothing sunlight. It's a haven of rest for weary travelers.

Each tree stands like a wooden pillar—firm and immovable. Oxygen fills the air. The ecosystem thrives. And peace floods your soul. Does this description of a forest remind you of God's plan for His people?

It does me! Just as individual trees grow, God calls Christians to grow. And like a forest, we are to mature as a body of believers, becoming strong and stable, giving life to a weary world.

*What about you?*
*Are you growing in the Lord?*
*Does living a fruitful life seem impossible?*

Maybe you feel your life is broken beyond repair. If so, there is hope! Jesus redeems broken lives. He makes all things new through the power of the gospel and His Word.

Just look at God's promises:

> "I will be like the dew to Israel;
> he shall blossom like the lily;
> he shall take root like the trees of Lebanon;
> his shoots shall spread out; his beauty shall be like the olive,
> and his fragrance like Lebanon.
> They shall return and dwell beneath my shadow;
> they shall flourish like the grain."
> **Hosea 14:5–7**

My desire for you as you read through this devotional is twofold:

1. That you will pay close attention to the Scriptures listed for each day—praying them back to God as sweet-smelling incense before His throne (Revelation 5:8). In His time, He will answer.

2. That you will dig deeper—taking time to read more of God's Word. His Word surpasses anything this world has to offer. He will revive your heart and satisfy your soul. You will not be disappointed.

So, let's begin . . . washed in His blood, clothed in His righteousness, let's pray:

> "Until the Spirit is poured upon us from on high,
> and the wilderness becomes a fruitful field,
> and the fruitful field is deemed a forest."
> **Isaiah 32:15**

## PART I
### Enjoy New Life

Day 1: Repent and Believe: The Broken Life
Day 2: Say No to Sin: The Crucified Life
Day 3: Say Yes to God: The Surrendered Life

## PART II
### Deepen Your Roots

Day 4: Understand the Depth of God's Love
Day 5: Study the Scriptures
Day 6: Meditate on Scripture

## PART III
### Fight Pests, Predators, & Diseases

Day 7: Know and Confess Sin
Day 8: Pursue Holiness
Day 9: Hate Sin
Day 10: Keep a Clean Mind
Day 11: Flee Sexual Immorality
Day 12: Fellowship in the Church
Day 13: Forgive Others
Day 14: Beware of Idleness
Day 15: Beware of Idolatry

## PART IV
### Bear Fruit

Day 16: Walk in the Spirit
Day 17: Pursue Love
Day 18: Pursue Humility
Day 19: Speak for the Glory of God
Day 20: Work for the Glory of God
Day 21: Sow Gospel Seeds
Day 22: Seek to Serve
Day 23: Use Your Spiritual Gifts

## PART V
### Weather the Storms

Day 24: Believe That God Is Sovereign
Day 25: Stand Firm in Your Faith
Day 26: Submit to God's Will
Day 27: Rejoice and Give Thanks
Day 28: Pray Continually
Day 29: Fear God and Obey
Day 30: Be Still and Wait
Day 31: Prepare for Heaven

Conclusion
Money Verses
Action Points
Additional Hymns
Acknowledgments
Notes

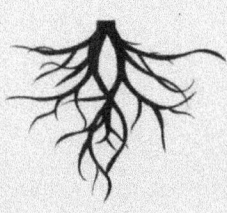

## PART I
*Enjoy New Life*

# Repent and Believe
## *The Broken Life*

*Day 1*

Resting beneath an oak tree calms the mind and soothes the soul. These gentle giants provide a quiet place to unwind, a place of peace for generations.

But you better wear shoes! In a boom year, these trees explode with acorns.[2] Thousands of hard nuts will drop and scatter everywhere.

These small seeds may seem insignificant, but they are packed with potential. Not only do they sustain wildlife, but according to God's design, select seeds will germinate. The outer shell breaks open, and new life springs forth. Over time, these tiny acorns transform into mighty oaks—a blessing to the world.

### *How are we like the acorn?*

Like a seed lying helpless on the ground, all of us are born dead in sin, separated from God, and unable to save ourselves.

But God loves us and performed the greatest miracle of all. He sent His Son, Jesus, to die on the cross to pay the penalty for our sins. Three days later, God raised Him from the dead. Now, whoever believes in Jesus and repents of their sin will be saved (Mark 1:15).

God rescues helpless sinners and forgives them. Do you believe this? If so, have you turned from your sin and put your trust in Christ? Ask Him for mercy right now. Nothing is impossible with God. He who transforms an ordinary seed into a living tree can likewise change you into a new creation (2 Corinthians 5:17).

# Verses to Pray and Ponder

"For God so loved the world,
that he gave his only Son,
that whoever believes in him
should not perish but have eternal life."
### John 3:16

"And it shall come to pass that everyone
who calls upon the name of the Lord shall be saved."
### Acts 2:21

"Repent therefore, and turn back,
that your sins may be blotted out,
that times of refreshing may come
from the presence of the Lord."
### Acts 3:19-20

"Turn to me and be saved,
all the ends of the earth!
For I am God, and there is no other."
### Isaiah 45:22

## Prayer for the Day

*Lord,*
Have mercy!
Set the captives free.
Open our eyes to see You.
In Your kindness,
draw us to Yourself.
Give us faith.
Grant us repentance.
Forgive our sins.
You alone can save.
In Your name
and for Your glory,
*Amen.*

**Hymn for the Day: Love Lifted Me**

# Say No to Sin
## *The Crucified Life*

*Day 2*

Gazing at an oak tree with its massive trunk, brawny branches, and countless leaves, you might never consider the shell from which it came. If you search for that tiny acorn, you won't find it. It's gone.

As you can see in this picture, when a tree begins, the shell of the seed dies, disintegrates, and never reconstitutes. Not so for us. When we repent and turn from our sins, we have new life in Christ, but the outer shell stays with us. Until our final day, we are stuck in this earthly tent called "flesh," and our flesh causes problems.

The desires of our flesh do not align with the desires of the Spirit, so the two battle. They wage war against one another, and the flesh doesn't die easily (Romans 7:18). It is stubborn and resists the Holy Spirit who indwells every believer. Therefore, we must learn to put to death the deeds of the flesh (Romans 8:13). If we don't, we will bear bad fruit. But this is a struggle, impossible for us in our own strength. The good news is that we have someone who understands and promises to help.

Jesus came to earth in human flesh and was tempted in all things as we are. Yet, He lived a perfect life. In every temptation, Jesus obeyed. Now, through the power of His Holy Spirit, He is ready to live His resurrected life through us. He will help us. In our weakness, He is strong (2 Corinthians 12:9).

### *Are you wrestling with stubborn sin?*

Run to Jesus. Draw near to Him through prayer (Mark 14:38). Hide His Word in your heart (Psalm 119:11). Pray for an accountability partner. When we confess our sins to one another and pray for one another, we break the power of sin. Confession brings healing (James 5:16).

Beloved, let's fight the good fight. As we do, God will give us grace and mercy to help in times of need (Hebrews 4:14–16). He will empower us to crucify the flesh and walk in His Spirit (Galatians 2:20).

# Verses to Pray and Ponder

"If anyone would come after me,
let him deny himself and take up his cross daily and follow me."
**Luke 9:23**

"And those who belong to Christ Jesus
have crucified the flesh with its passions and desires."
**Galatians 5:24**

"But far be it from me to boast except in the cross of our Lord Jesus Christ,
by which the world has been crucified to me, and I to the world."
**Galatians 6:14**

"But thanks be to God, that you who were once slaves of sin
have become obedient from the heart."
**Romans 6:17**

"I have been crucified with Christ. It is no longer I who live,
but Christ who lives in me. And the life I now live in the flesh I live by faith
in the Son of God, who loved me and gave himself for me."
**Galations 2:20**

"All things are lawful for me, but not all things are profitable.
All things are lawful for me, but I will not be mastered by anything."
**1 Corinthians 6:12 NASB1995**

## Prayer for the Day

*Lord,*
Give us victory over sin.
Help us to deny ourselves,
take up our cross,
and follow You.
Help us walk in Your resurrection power.
Lead us not into temptation
but deliver us from evil.
In Your name
and for Your glory,
*Amen.*

**Hymn for the Day: Wherever He Leads I'll Go**

# Say Yes to God
## *The Surrendered Life*

*Day 3*

In the 1630s, John Endecott, the first governor of the Massachusetts Bay Colony, planted a pear sapling. According to legend, as he planted the tree, Endecott said to his children, "No doubt when we have gone, the tree will still be alive."[3] John Endecott was right. Almost 400 years later, the tree still bears fruit.

And not only in Massachusetts. From cuttings, the tree bears fruit in seventeen other states![4]

### *What can we learn from the Endecott Pear Tree?*

The death of one ordinary seed has the potential to bear fruit and bless the world for generations.

Christianity is not a casual commitment. It requires self-abandonment—death to our will and our way. But many times, we reject God's reign. We don't trust Him, so we cling to our comforts, desires, and dreams. By doing so, we quench the Spirit and fail to bear lasting fruit.

### *Are you resisting Him?*
### *Are you clinging to your selfish desires?*

God is a kind, tender Father. He loves you. You can trust Him. Surrendering to His plan—a better one than yours—will have far-reaching results, yielding greater fruitfulness and greater rewards.

Maybe God's plan doesn't make sense to you at the present time. Maybe it looks foolish and fruitless. Do not fear. God is wise and knows what He is doing. Be faithful in every season. In due time, you will bear an abundance of fruit.

# Verses to Pray and Ponder

"Truly, truly, I say to you,
unless a grain of wheat falls into the earth and dies,
it remains alone;
but if it dies, it bears much fruit."
### John 12:24

"Father, if you are willing,
remove this cup from me.
Nevertheless, not my will, but yours, be done."
### Luke 22:42

"For whoever would save his life will lose it,
but whoever loses his life for my sake and the gospel's will save it."
### Mark 8:35

"But whatever gain I had,
I counted as loss for the sake of Christ.
Indeed, I count everything as loss because of the surpassing worth
of knowing Christ Jesus my Lord."
### Philippians 3:7–8

## Prayer for the Day

*Lord,*

Help us!
Make us wholly devoted,
fully surrendered
—abandoned to Your will—
so that You can bear fruit in and through our lives.
Now and in the generations to come.
In Jesus's name,

*Amen.*

**Hymn for the Day: I Surrender All**

## PART II
### Deepen Your Roots

# Understand the Depth of God's Love

*Day 4*

The first root that sprouts from an acorn is the taproot.[5] This vital root digs into the soil, anchors the seedling, and supplies nutrients to the tiny tree. If the seedling survives, the taproot will evolve into a rugged root, helping stabilize the tree for years.

*The love of God is the taproot of the Christian life.*

And it's a deep root! It's immovable, unshakable, and keeps us anchored amid our deepest trials.

Let's explore the depth of God's love. Although we were born His enemies:
- He chose us before the foundation of the world (Ephesians 1:4).
- He sent His Son to die for us (John 3:16).
- He knitted us together in our mother's womb (Psalm 139:13).
- He created us for a purpose (Ephesians 2:10).

Then, in His time and according to His plan:
- He pursued us (John 6:44).
- He rescued us (Colossians 1:13).
- He delivered us from sin (Romans 8:2; John 8:36).
- He seated us with Him in the heavenly places (Ephesians 2:1–6).
- He clothed us in His righteousness (Isaiah 61:10).
- He made us citizens of heaven, coheirs with Christ (Philippians 3:20; Romans 8:16–17).

Nothing will separate us from the love of God (Romans 8:35–39). Now and forever, we are safe and secure, hidden in the depth of His love (Colossians 3:3).

*Isn't God amazing?*

Let's embrace these golden nuggets until they become our identity, the core of who we are. They will keep us rooted and grounded enough to endure every storm.

# Verses to Pray and Ponder

"So we have come to know and to believe
the love that God has for us."
**1 John 4:16**

"But God shows his love for us in that
while we were still sinners,
Christ died for us."
**Romans 5:8**

"For you formed my inward parts;
you knitted me together in my mother's womb.
I praise you, for I am fearfully and wonderfully made."
**Psalm 139:13–14**

"For we are his workmanship,
created in Christ Jesus for good works,
which God prepared beforehand,
that we should walk in them."
**Ephesians 2:10**

"The steadfast love of the LORD never ceases;
his mercies never come to an end;
they are new every morning;
great is your faithfulness."
**Lamentations 3:22–23**

## Prayer for the Day

*Lord,*
Overwhelm us.
Awaken our senses to the knowledge of Your love.
It is higher than the heavens;
it is deeper than the sea.
Pour Your love into our hearts,
and let it overflow for Your glory
and the blessing of others.
In Jesus's name,
*Amen.*

**Hymn for the Day: O the Deep, Deep Love of Jesus**

# Study the Scriptures

Day 5

Have you ever noticed roots bulging from the base of an oak tree? Once the taproot is established, lateral roots develop and become the tree's primary anchor.[6] These roots can spread four to seven times the circumference of the tree's crown.

On the tips of these roots are tiny root hairs that soak up water and nutrients from the soil. As they do, the root system expands and nourishes the tree. Over time, a robust root system will produce a healthy tree with an enormous crown.[7]

God desires His children to become mighty oaks, glorifying Him and blessing others. But to flourish, we need an extensive root system.

Like tree roots seeking nourishment, we must seek wisdom, knowledge, and understanding. The more truth we absorb, the more our roots will expand, empowering us to mature and bear an abundance of fruit.

*Are you digging into God's Word?*

Light devotional reading is good. But, digging deeper is better. Rearrange your priorities, say no to lesser things, and create time to study God's Word.

In time, as we grow in wisdom, God will transform us into a mighty oak of righteousness, a blessing to this weary world (Isaiah 61:1-3).

# Verses to Pray and Ponder

"It is written,
'Man shall not live by bread alone,
but by every word that comes from the mouth of God.'"
**Matthew 4:4**

"Buy truth, and do not sell it;
buy wisdom, instruction, and understanding."
**Proverbs 23:23**

"The law of your mouth is better to me
than thousands of gold and silver pieces."
**Psalm 119:72**

"Your words were found, and I ate them,
and your words became to me a joy
and the delight of my heart."
**Jeremiah 15:16**

"If you turn at my reproof, behold,
I will pour out my spirit to you;
I will make my words known to you."
**Proverbs 1:23**

## Prayer for the Day

*Lord,*
We are so distracted.
Incline our hearts to Your instruction.
Magnify Your Word and make it glorious.
Open our eyes to behold wonderful things.
Permit us to mature into mighty oaks of righteousness,
deeply rooted, full of wisdom,
knowledge, and understanding
—for Your glory alone.
In Jesus's name,
*Amen.*

## Hymn for the Day: How Firm a Foundation

# Meditate on Scripture

*Day 6*

Weeping willows are fascinating trees. Their branches bow like an umbrella, dangle with grace, and display delightful colors. They sparkle with green in the spring and radiate gold in the fall.[8] These trees bring beauty, shade, and sanctuary for hurried lives and weary souls.

However, if you plant a weeping willow, beware.[9] They need lots of water! Because of their thirsty root systems, they will forage into your sewage system and water lines, aggressively searching for water.

For best results, plant willows by streams or ponds where their roots can be nourished. With a continual flow of water, the tree will be happy and healthy for years.

Christians, like willows, need an endless flow of water—living water from God's Word. Without it, our hearts gravitate to worthless things, causing severe problems.

*How do you quench your soul's thirst?*

*Are you sipping water from the world?*

*Or are you drinking clean water from God's Word?*

Just as the roots of a willow drink from a pond, let's draw continually from God's fountain of fresh water (Jeremiah 2:13). It will delight our hearts and satisfy our souls. We will flourish and bear fruit, even in this dry land.

# Verses to Pray and Ponder

"Oh how I love your law!
It is my meditation all the day."
**Psalm 119:97**

"This Book of the Law shall not depart from your mouth,
but you shall meditate on it day and night,
so that you may be careful to do according to all that is written in it.
For then you will make your way prosperous,
and then you will have good success."
**Joshua 1:8**

"Blessed is the man who walks not in the counsel of the wicked,
nor stands in the way of sinners,
nor sits in the seat of scoffers;
but his delight is in the law of the LORD,
and on his law he meditates day and night.
He is like a tree planted by streams of water
that yields its fruit in its season,
and its leaf does not wither.
In all that he does, he prospers."
**Psalm 1:1–3**

## Prayer for the Day

*Lord,*
We love Your law!
It's sweet and satisfying.
Help us to delight in every word,
meditating day and night
so that we can prosper and bear fruit.
Thank You that as we abide in You
and Your words abide in us,
You hear our prayers.
In Jesus's name,
*Amen.*

**Hymn for the Day: Wonderful Words of Life**

## PART III
# Fight Pests, Predators, & Diseases

# Know and Confess Sin

*Day 7*

Every spring, our family enjoyed a dogwood tree teeming with snow-white blossoms. This delightful tree decorated our yard for many years.

But one day, we looked at the tree more closely and saw a different story. Hidden beneath the leaves was fungi,[10] a hotbed of disease. How did we miss it? Sadly, the tree was languishing, so we excavated it with a chain and backhoe.

What can we learn from this? At first glance, trees may look healthy, but inside, they can be infested with disease. Without careful inspection and timely treatment, trees can wither and die.[11]

As Christians, we, too, are vulnerable to pests and diseases. Our flesh, the world, and the devil relentlessly attack our spiritual health. Unless we watch over our souls carefully, sin creeps in, deceives our minds, and hardens our hearts. Like pests on a tree left unchecked, sin can devastate our lives.

*How do we keep watch?*

*How can we prevent spiritual decay?*

Thank God for His Word. As we read Scripture, He opens our eyes, exposes our sins, and reveals evil intentions. And then, when we confess our sins, He immediately forgives us. He tosses our sins into the heart of the sea and remembers them no more.

Are you amazed? Jesus's blood is powerful. It's sufficient to remove every sin: big, little, and repeated. No matter how ugly our sins are, when we repent, His blood washes us white as snow (Isaiah 1:18). Do you allow time for God to search your heart? Read God's Word daily. Ask Him to convict you of sin and expose any wickedness. Become aware of your sin patterns.

Then, as you go through your day, let ongoing, silent confession before the Lord be your moment-by-moment practice. Confession frees us. It cleanses us. It keeps us in fellowship with God.

# Verses to Pray and Ponder

"If we say we have no sin,
we deceive ourselves,
and the truth is not in us.
If we confess our sins,
he is faithful and just to forgive us our sins
and to cleanse us from all unrighteousness."

**1 John 1:8–9**

"Whoever conceals his transgressions will not prosper,
but he who confesses and forsakes them will obtain mercy."

**Proverbs 28:13**

"If I had cherished iniquity in my heart, the Lord would not have listened."

**Psalm 66:18**

"And when he comes,
he will convict the world concerning sin
and righteousness and judgment."

**John 16:8**

"Who can discern his errors?
Declare me innocent from hidden faults.
Keep back your servant also from presumptuous sins;
let them not have dominion over me."

**Psalm 19:12–13**

## Prayer for the Day

*Lord,*
Have mercy.
Help us to see and know our sins.
Convict us and grant us repentance.
Create in us a clean heart.
Wash us whiter than snow.
Restore the joy of our salvation,
so that we may teach sinners Your ways
and declare Your mighty deeds.
We ask in Your name,
*Amen.*

**Hymn for the Day: Nothing but the Blood**

# Pursue Holiness

*Day 8*

Next time you walk through a forest, notice the trees bending toward a clearing. These trees yearn for light.[12]

Despite the pull of gravity, once a seedling sprouts, a tree grows upward in pursuit of light. God engineered this miracle by mixing auxin into the DNA of seedlings. This hormone elongates the stem cells and causes them to bend in the direction of light.

God, likewise, instills into the DNA of each new believer a spiritual yearning for His light. Instead of hunkering down in the darkness of sin, we hunger to be holy as He is holy (Matthew 5:48)—to walk in the light as He is in the light (1 John 1:5–7; Ephesians 5:8).

But unfortunately, our fleshly appetites sometimes overpower and extinguish our pursuit of holiness. Understanding the weakness of our flesh, God gives us an answer to this problem. Like the branches of a tree bend toward light,[13] we must keep turning toward God and the light of His Word.

As we fix our eyes on Jesus, He will turn our hearts to hunger for holiness. He will cause us to hate the darkness. And His holiness will become our passion, our greatest desire.

*How do you spend your time?*

*Are you entangled in worldly pursuits?*

Turn your eyes upon God and feed on His Word. As you do, He will loosen the chains that bind you and set your heart ablaze with holy fire that yearns for His holiness.

# Verses to Pray and Ponder

"One thing have I asked of the LORD,
that will I seek after . . .
to gaze upon the beauty of the LORD
and to inquire in his temple."
**PSALM 27:4**

"Blessed are those who hunger and thirst for righteousness."
**MATTHEW 5:6**

"As a deer pants for flowing streams,
so pants my soul for you, O God.
My soul thirsts for God,
for the living God."
**PSALM 42:1–2**

"You have said, 'Seek my face.'
My heart says to you,
'Your face, LORD, do I seek.'"
**PSALM 27:8**

"There is nothing on earth that I desire besides you."
**PSALM 73:25**

"But seek first the kingdom of God and his righteousness,
and all these things will be added to you."
**MATTHEW 6:33**

## Prayer for the Day

*Lord,*
We are deceived and distracted by this world.
Today, turn our hearts to pursue Your holiness.
Deliver us from youthful passions and vain pursuits.
Become our one desire,
the one thing we seek after.
We ask in Your name
and for Your glory,
*Amen.*

**Hymn for the Day: Take Time to Be Holy**

# Hate Sin

*Day 9*

Unlike people, trees are stationary. If predators attack, trees are stuck and unable to flee. Yet God, in His wisdom, gave them defense mechanisms. Some are structural, such as thorns. But some are chemical—yes, chemical warfare! When predators threaten the life of some trees, these trees emit a chemical to defend themselves.

One such tree is the acacia, which giraffes love to eat. When these long-necked mammals nibble on their leaves, the acacia releases tannins, a powerful chemical that makes the leaves distasteful and deters the giraffes from eating them.[14]

As Christians, we live in a wicked world surrounded by a predator called sin. Every day, dangers from within and without threaten our ability to bear fruit. But God has provided a way of escape: His Word. As the chemicals defend the acacia from predators, the Word of God protects us from sin.

*Is sin crouching at your door?*

*Are you tempted to sin?*

If you are like me, resisting sin is a daily struggle.

Let's spend time in God's Word. As Holy Scripture saturates our hearts and minds, we begin to hate sin. We learn to recognize evil and are better equipped to defend ourselves.

Praise God for His gracious provision. May His Word dwell richly within us so we can flourish, even among our enemies—the world, the flesh, and the devil.

# Verses to Pray and Ponder

"Abhor what is evil;
cling to what is good."
**ROMANS 12:9 NASB1995**

"You [Christ] have loved righteousness
and hated wickedness."
**HEBREWS 1:9**

"O you who love the LORD,
hate evil."
**PSALM 97:10**

"I hate and abhor falsehood,
but I love your law."
**PSALM 119:163**

"The fear of the LORD is hatred of evil.
Pride and arrogance and the way of evil and perverted speech I hate."
**PROVERBS 8:13**

## Prayer for the Day

*Lord,*
Thank You for the power of Your Word.
Protect us from sin.
Cause us to abhor what is evil
and cling to what is good.
Cause us to love what You love
and hate what You hate.
Thank You for accomplishing what concerns us.
In Jesus's name,
*Amen.*

**Hymn for the Day: A Mighty Fortress Is Our God**

# Keep a Clean Mind

*Day 10*

Nestled among the trees in eastern Alabama sits Auburn University. Auburn is a sprawling campus steeped in tradition and home to an army of devoted die-hard sports fans.

One of Auburn's most famous traditions is celebrating football victories by rolling two live oak trees with toilet paper. These beloved oaks sit at the university entrance, known as Toomer's Corner. After each victory, fans toss toilet paper through the air and wrap the trees in a celebratory fashion.

However, this tradition was threatened in 2010 when a man poisoned the two oaks with Spike 80DF, an herbicide known for killing trees.[15] The university tried to save them, but the dose was fatal, and the trees were destined to die. The university had no choice but to uproot them.[16]

It was a tearful day for Auburn University.

### *What can we learn from this tragedy?*

As believers, God declares us holy. We are chosen vessels set apart to bear fruit and bring Him glory. But Satan despises us for our purpose and targets our minds with poison. Just as a little herbicide can limit a tree's ability to bear fruit, so can the devil's lies pollute our minds and render us useless to the kingdom of God (John 10:10).

Therefore, protect your mind from poison. Be careful what you look at and who you listen to. Close your eyes (Psalm 101:3) and cover your ears to anything corrupt (Matthew 6:22–23).

Above all, dwell on Scripture, day and night. The Word washes away Satan's lies and purifies our thought life.

Keeping a clean mind is a daily battle, but a battle worth fighting. By His grace, let's be diligent. Let's guard our minds so that we can bear fruit and be useful in the kingdom of God.

# Verses to Pray and Ponder

"Be sober-minded; be watchful. Your adversary the devil prowls around
like a roaring lion, seeking someone to devour."
**1 Peter 5:8**

"Resist the devil, and he will flee from you."
**James 4:7**

"We destroy arguments and every lofty opinion
raised against the knowledge of God,
and take every thought captive to obey Christ."
**2 Corinthians 10:5**

"Set your minds on things that are above,
not on things that are on earth."
**Colossians 3:2**

"Finally, brothers, whatever is true . . . honorable . . .
just . . . pure . . . lovely . . . commendable,
if there is any excellence . . . anything worthy of praise,
think about these things."
**Philippians 4:8**

"You keep him in perfect peace whose mind is stayed on you,
because he trusts in you."
**Isaiah 26:3**

## Prayer for the Day

*Lord,*
It's hard to control our thoughts.
Our imaginations run wild.
Have mercy!
Keep our minds focused on You and Your Word.
Help us to reject evil thoughts and Satan's lies
so we can bear fruit in Your name
and for Your glory,
*Amen.*

**Hymn for the Day: Like a River Glorious**

# Flee Sexual Immorality

**Day 11**

Giant sequoia trees tower over the Sierra Nevada mountain range in northern California. They are the largest, most stately trees on earth. They can live thousands of years, grow 300 feet high, and extend over 30 feet wide. For this reason, they are called nature's skyscrapers.

*What is the key to the sequoia's success?*
*How do they endure the forest fires?*

The answer is their bark. God created sequoias with a resilient, fibrous bark that grows up to two feet thick. As a result, even in a raging forest fire, the sequoias typically survive.[17]

While sequoias often battle forest fires, Christians often experience sexual temptations. But God has provided a way for us to endure these fiery temptations: the Word of God.

The truths of God's Word are like bark that enables us to withstand temptation. Therefore, we must strengthen our hearts with Scripture, memorize it, and meditate on it. As we do, the Holy Spirit weaves it into every fiber of our being. Over time, our "bark" will thicken and protect us in every blazing trial.

Sexual temptations abound, so prepare:
- Think about situations where you experience temptation. Are there things or people you need to avoid (Romans 13:14)?
- Meet with a mature, godly friend for weekly confession and accountability (James 5:16).
- Keep fellowship with like-minded believers (1 Corinthians 5:11, 15:33).
- Pray (Matthew 26:41).

So that when fiery temptations come, you will not only survive but flourish. You will reflect the purity and holiness of God in this harsh, provocative world (1 Corinthians 10:13).

# Verses to Pray and Ponder

"Flee from sexual immorality . . .
do you not know that your body is a temple of the Holy Spirit within you . . .
So glorify God in your body."
**1 Corinthians 6:18–20**

"Put on the Lord Jesus Christ,
and make no provision for the flesh,
to gratify its desires."
**Romans 13:14**

"For this is the will of God . . . that you abstain from sexual immorality;
that each one of you know how to control his own body in holiness and honor."
**1 Thessalonians 4:3–4**

"But sexual immorality . . . must not even be named among you,
as is proper among saints."
**Ephesians 5:3**

"Let marriage be held in honor among all,
and let the marriage bed be undefiled,
for God will judge the sexually immoral and adulterous."
**Hebrews 13:4**

"You [are] not to associate with anyone who bears the name of brother
if he is guilty of sexual immorality."
**1 Corinthians 5:11**

## Prayer for the Day

*Lord,*
Thank You for living a perfect life on our behalf.
We come as beggars to Your throne.
Give us mercy and grace to help in times of need.
Help us to walk with integrity in our homes.
Help us to crucify our passions and evil desires.
Fill us with Your Spirit and give us victory over sexual sin.
One day at a time.
One step at a time.
For Your glory,
*Amen.*

**Hymn for the Day: Victory in Jesus**

# Fellowship in the Church

*Day 12*

Woodlands can appear as overgrown tracts of land, with each tree competing for resources and seeking to monopolize the landscape. But scientific research reveals something different.

Forests are actually a unified body of trees. They support one another, live in harmony, and function as a single organism.[18]

How is this possible? Trees connect through mycelium, an underground fungal network scientists call the "wood wide web."[19] Just as people communicate online, trees communicate with one another. They send warnings of disease, drought, and coming dangers.

Even more fascinating is that when one tree is suffering, another tree will provide the resources it needs to thrive. For example, when a sapling dwells in the shadow of a mature tree without exposure to the sun, the older tree (called the mother tree) will nurture and feed the younger tree.

All creation glorifies God, and trees are no exception. God designed trees to need each other in order to mature into a fruitful forest.

God designed Christians the same way. We need each other to mature into the image of Christ.

When we connect with fellow believers, we can survive drought, weather storms, and fight diseases. It's a means of exponential growth. In contrast, living alone hinders our growth and leads to spiritual weakness.

*How is your soul today?*

*Are you struggling?*

*Are you trying to live the Christian life alone?*

Join a healthy church where you can connect with mature believers. Only then can you enjoy the riches of God's grace and flourish with other Christians like a forest of life-giving trees.

# Verses to Pray and Ponder

"I am a companion of all who fear you,
of those who keep your precepts."
**Psalm 119:63**

"Whoever walks with the wise becomes wise,
but the companion of fools will suffer harm."
**Proverbs 13:20**

"Do not be deceived:
'Bad company ruins good morals.'"
**1 Corinthians 15:33**

"So flee youthful passions and pursue righteousness . . .
along with those who call upon the Lord from a pure heart."
**2 Timothy 2:22**

"Iron sharpens iron,
and one man sharpens another."
**Proverbs 27:17**

# Prayer for the Day

*Lord,*
Thank You for the church and godly companions.
Make us one.
Give us the mind of Christ and the love of Christ.
Knit our hearts together.
Use us to strengthen, encourage, and sharpen one another.
In this wilderness, make us a life-giving forest, an oasis,
and a source of refreshment for those in need.
In Jesus's name,
*Amen.*

**Hymn for the Day: Onward Christian Soldiers**

# Forgive Others

**Day 13**

Few things frighten homeowners like the sight of termites. Termite damage can be devastating. One of the most destructive termites is the Formosan termite. While most termites prefer dead wood, Formosan termites delight in living trees.

In a few short months, one nest can hollow out a tree devouring it one bite at a time. It's no wonder these pests are known as the silent destroyers.[20] Left undetected, they will spread and destroy nearby trees and even homes.[21]

Unforgiveness is like a termite infestation. As wood invites termites, unforgiveness invites bitterness. Bitterness will decay our inner man, causing us to produce rotten fruit. Instead of walking in wholeness and strength, we simmer in anger.

But the damage doesn't end there. As termites spread from tree to tree, our bitterness can spread to those around us. Soon, it will infect the people we love—our families, friends, church, and coworkers.

Do not be deceived. All Christians can be silently destroyed by the termites of unforgiveness. So, let's examine our lives for signs of an unforgiving heart, such as anger, self-pity, jealousy, gossip, slander, and a critical spirit.

Difficult people and deep trials will come into our lives.

*How will we respond?*

*Will we forgive, or will we harbor hurts?*

The good news is that God doesn't hold grudges. When we confess our sins, He forgives us. He remembers our sin no more. And He will help us. God will empower us to forgive and flourish as life-giving trees. Praise Him for His amazing grace.

# Verses to Pray and Ponder

"Blessed are the merciful,
for they shall receive mercy."
**MATTHEW 5:7**

"Be kind to one another,
tenderhearted, forgiving one another,
as God in Christ forgave you."
**EPHESIANS 4:32**

"Bearing with one another and,
if one has a complaint against another,
forgiving each other; as the Lord has forgiven you,
so you also must forgive."
**COLOSSIANS 3:13**

"Good sense makes one slow to anger,
and it is his glory to overlook an offense."
**PROVERBS 19:11**

"Do not be overcome by evil,
but overcome evil with good."
**ROMANS 12:21**

## Prayer for the Day

*Lord,*
You freely forgive.
You wash away our sins
and remember them no more.
Empower us to do likewise.
Help us to say as You said,
"Father, forgive them, for they know not what they do" (Luke 23:34).
And as Joseph said, "You meant evil against me,
but God meant it for good" (Genesis 50:20).
In Jesus's name,
*Amen.*

## Hymn for the Day: Amazing Grace

# Beware of Idleness

*Day 14*

Tumbleweeds! Growing up in West Texas, I remember seeing these weeds adorned in white lights and sprayed with fake snow at Christmastime. They were unique and useful for the holidays, but typically, tumbleweeds are a nuisance.[22]

While most trees establish roots and bear fruit, the tumbleweed, also known as the Russian thistle, is the opposite.[23] It begins as bright green grass-like shoots, but within six months, the shoots perish and morph into a skeleton, a ball of brittle twigs that causes trouble.[24]

With one gust of wind, they uproot and roll aimlessly through pastures and neighborhoods. They create hazardous road conditions, destroy crops, and trigger fires.[25]

Like the Russian thistle, our lives are brief. We are here today and gone tomorrow. But God didn't design us to be a tumbleweed and roll aimlessly through life. He created us to be mighty oaks with a unique purpose. Therefore, while we can, let's establish deep roots in God's Word and live with intention.

*How do you spend your time?*

Do you find yourself sidetracked, wasting time on things that don't matter? Do you click on something online and get derailed for hours? Laziness is a sin that can lead to greater sin, causing trouble for ourselves and those around us.

Soon, our days will end, and we will have to give an account of how we spent our time. While we can, let's dig into God's Word, expand our roots, and do God's will. In time, we will bear fruit and leave this world with no regrets.

# Verses to Pray and Ponder

"Sow your seed in the morning and do not be idle in the evening."
**ECCLESIASTES 11:6 NASB**

"Jesus said to them,
'My food is to do the will of him who sent me
and to accomplish his work.'"
**JOHN 4:34**

"We must work the works of him who sent me while it is day;
night is coming, when no one can work."
**JOHN 9:4**

"No soldier gets entangled in civilian pursuits,
since his aim is to please the one who enlisted him."
**2 TIMOTHY 2:4**

"Look carefully then how you walk,
not as unwise but as wise, making the best use of the time,
because the days are evil.
Therefore do not be foolish,
but understand what the will of the Lord is."
**EPHESIANS 5:15–17**

## Prayer for the Day

*Lord,*
Thank You for this brief moment on earth.
Our days are a passing shadow, a mere breath.
Do not let us waste one day.
Deliver us from distractions.
Make us faithful in the little things.
Make us sober-minded and self-controlled.
Make us disciplined and diligent to do your will.
In Jesus's name,
*Amen.*

**Hymn for the Day: Stand Up, Stand Up for Jesus**

# Beware of Idolatry

*Day 15*

God designed trees to bear fruit and bless the world. But sometimes, a rogue shoot, called a sucker, will emerge from the base of the trunk and prevent the tree from flourishing.[26]

These shoots may seem harmless, but if neglected, they suck the life out of the tree. Arborists tell us to yank them up from their roots or, if they are too embedded, cut them out with sharp pruning tools.[27]

Suckers on a tree are much like idols in our hearts. They are subtle. What begins as a harmless desire soon turns into a craving, an obsession—something we covet; something we desire more than God; something we spend an excessive amount of time, energy, and resources to obtain. This could be a relationship, money, or a desire to be accepted by others.

Be careful. In every season, idols sneak in, but especially in seasons of disappointment. Instead of turning to Christ, we easily turn to the world to deaden the pain or find an escape. Think about it. Is your heart lukewarm toward God? If so, there may be an idol hidden in your heart.

*What occupies your mind? What dominates your time?*

*Is there something or someone you treasure more than Christ?*

Take heed. The consequences of serving idols are devastating. They steal your joy, rob your peace, waste your time, deplete your energy, squander your money, and destroy your relationships. If left unchecked, they cause sorrow for you and those around you (Psalm 16:4).

Let's ask God to search our hearts and reveal any idols. Let's do whatever it takes to walk in freedom: remove them (Romans 13:14), memorize Scripture, seek counsel and accountability.

God is a jealous God. He wants our whole hearts. Turn to Him, and He will heal you. He will transform you into a life-giving tree, free and fruitful for His glory and the blessing of others.

# Verses to Pray and Ponder

"You shall have no other gods before me."
**EXODUS 20:3**

"Little children, keep yourselves from idols."
**1 JOHN 5:21**

"I will sprinkle clean water on you,
and you shall be clean from all your uncleannesses,
and from all your idols I will cleanse you."
**EZEKIEL 36:25**

"Turn my eyes from looking at worthless things;
and give me life in your ways."
**PSALM 119:37**

"For they themselves report . . .
how you turned to God from idols to serve the living and true God."
**1 THESSALONIANS 1:9**

"They shall not defile themselves anymore
with their idols and their detestable things. . .
But I will save them from all the backslidings in which they have sinned,
and will cleanse them; and they shall be my people,
and I will be their God."
**EZEKIEL 37:23**

## Prayer for the Day

*Lord,*
Have mercy.
Our hearts are divided.
Sometimes we love the world and the things of the world
more than we love You.
Today, let rivers of mercy flow from Your throne.
Restore us.
Uproot our idols.
Give us hearts wholly devoted to You.
Become our one passion,
our one desire.
In Jesus's name,
*Amen.*

## Hymn for the Day: Whiter Than Snow

## PART IV
## Bear Fruit

# Walk in the Spirit

**Day 16**

In the morning, I love stepping outside, hearing the birds, marveling at the sky, and breathing in the fresh air. It reminds me of Psalm 150:6: "Let everything that has breath praise the Lord!"

God gives life to every creature. And He does it through trees.[28] Using photosynthesis, trees clean the air of carbon dioxide and release oxygen to the Earth. It's God's amazing design.[29]

Like God created trees to give physical life, in a similar way, He created believers to breathe spiritual life.

*How do we do this?*

Through the power of the Holy Spirit. When God saves us, He seals us with His Holy Spirit (Ephesians 1:13). Then, as we learn to walk in lockstep with the Lord, heavenly fruit springs forth from our lives. Jesus shines through us, and people are blessed.

*Do you desire to walk in the Spirit?*

I do! But living Spirit-filled is possible only when we are clean vessels. So, daily, let's bathe in the water of God's Word. Let's confess our sins, and ask Him to cleanse us of all unrighteousness (1 John 1:9). As we do, we are becoming prepared vessels, ready for service.

I often pray, "Lord, fill me. Use me. Live Your life through me." And He does, and He will!

Let's fully surrender to the Lord so that, like the sun empowers photosynthesis, the Holy Spirit will empower us to be life-givers—making our world a more joyful and peaceful place to live.

## Verses to Pray and Ponder

"But I say, walk by the Spirit,
and you will not carry out the desire of the flesh."
**GALATIANS 5:16 NASB**

"But the fruit of the Spirit is love, joy, peace, patience,
kindness, goodness, faithfulness, gentleness, self-control;
against such things there is no law."
**GALATIANS 5:22–23**

"And do not get drunk with wine . . . but be filled with the Spirit,
addressing one another in psalms and hymns and spiritual songs,
singing and making melody to the Lord with your heart,
giving thanks always and for everything . . .
submitting to one another out of reverence for Christ."
**EPHESIANS 5:18–21**

## Prayer for the Day

*Lord,*
Make us clean vessels
—holy temples—
so that Your Holy Spirit can fill us
and fully permeate our lives.
Make us life-giving,
joyful, and fruitful
even in this withering world.
We ask in Your name,
*Amen.*

**Hymn for the Day: Spirit of the Living God**

# Pursue Love

*Day 17*

Have you ever visited St. Augustine, Florida? It's our nation's oldest city, known for its blue skies, beautiful beaches, and rich history. If you visit, hop on a trolley and enjoy the city. You will bounce along brick streets, enjoy fresh pastries, and discover snippets of history.

While there, don't miss the "Love Trees." Scattered throughout the city, these seven pairs of trees grow in and through each other. Each tree is a different species, yet they embrace.[30]

Just as God can cause two trees to become one, He can do the same for His children. He can "knit us together" and make us one for His glory ( John 17:20–23; Psalm 133).

But we have a part to play. Loving people is impossible in our own strength. Therefore, we must draw near to God and ask Him for help. In the power of His Holy Spirit, we can love others, regardless of their deeds and differences (John 13:34–35).

Think about it.

*Do you genuinely love people?*

*Or do you pick and choose whom you will love?*

Pray and meditate on the following Scriptures until God's love is flowing through you to everyone everywhere.

And let's make it personal. Is there someone in your home, workplace, or church who needs love? This week, ask God to empower you to love that person as He loves you (1 John 4:19; Romans 13:8) and He will.

# Verses to Pray and Ponder

"Let love be genuine."
**ROMANS 12:9**

"Love one another with brotherly affection.
Outdo one another in showing honor."
**ROMANS 12:10**

"May the Lord make your love increase and overflow for each other
and for everyone else."
**1 THESSALONIANS 3:12 NIV**

"And above all these put on love,
which binds everything together in perfect harmony."
**COLOSSIANS 3:14**

"Above all, keep loving one another earnestly,
since love covers a multitude of sins."
**1 PETER 4:8**

"Love is patient and kind;
love does not envy or boast;
it is not arrogant or rude.
It does not insist on its own way;
it is not irritable or resentful . . .
Love bears all things, believes all things,
hopes all things, endures all things.
Love never ends."
**1 CORINTHIANS 13:4–5, 7–8**

## Prayer for the Day

*Lord,*
Your love is amazing!
You chose us and pursued us.
We were enemies, but You call us friends.
Fill us with Your Spirit
and empower us to love as You love
—genuinely, earnestly,
and unconditionally.
In Your name
and for Your glory,
*Amen.*

## Hymn for the Day: And Can It Be?

# Pursue Humility

*Day 18*

While most trees will overpower neighboring trees, some will defer or create space for others. This phenomenon is called crown shyness.[31] While researchers don't fully understand why some trees yield to one another, we can see it as a magnificent display of God's creative power.[32]

Depending on where you live, you may have to travel far to find this phenomenon. It's rare, existing mostly in tropical forests and remote places like Malaysia and Argentina.

Like crown shyness, genuine humility is a rare wonder. Only one man possessed perfect humility—Jesus Christ. Although He is God, He set aside His glory, emptied Himself, took on human flesh, and put others before Himself. In the ultimate display of humility, He died on the cross, taking our sin upon Himself so that we might live (2 Corinthians 5:21).

Jesus is our example, but walking in humility is not easy. As descendants of Adam, we were born proud. We crave attention, desire to be first, and yearn for glory.

*Do you wrestle with these things?*

Beware. Your heart will deceive you (Jeremiah 17:9), and the consequences of pride are devastating. Andrew Murray wrote, "There is nothing so natural to man, . . . so hidden from our sight, . . . so dangerous as pride."[33] He says it's "like a viper—-full of deadly poison."

Think about it. Pride is like a snake lurking in our hearts. It can control our thoughts, words, and deeds. And we don't even realize it. So, let's pursue humility. A good place to start is by meditating on passages such as Philippians 2:1–11 and Matthew 5:1–9.

These verses, hidden in our hearts, will empower us to:
- Prefer others.
- Serve without needing recognition.
- Desire God's glory and not our own.

Pursuing humility is a lifelong process, yet it's worth the effort. Over time, God's kindness and deference will flow from our hearts, people will be blessed, and God will be glorified.

# Verses to Pray and Ponder

"Humble yourselves, therefore,
under the mighty hand of God
so that at the proper time he may exalt you."
**1 Peter 5:6**

"When pride comes, then comes disgrace,
but with the humble is wisdom."
**Proverbs 11:2**

"Do nothing from selfish ambition or conceit,
but in humility count others more significant than yourselves."
**Philippians 2:3**

"The reward for humility and fear of the Lord is riches and honor and life."
**Proverbs 22:4**

"Do not be haughty, but associate with the lowly.
Never be wise in your own sight."
**Romans 12:16**

"It is not good to eat much honey,
nor is it glorious to seek one's own glory."
**Proverbs 25:27**

## Prayer for the Day

*Father,*
Forgive us.
We are proud.
Make us like Jesus, gentle and kind.
Make us broken and contrite,
content with weakness,
delighted to be nothing.
Help us to pursue Your glory and not our own.
In Jesus's name,
*Amen.*

**Hymn for the Day: When I Survey the Wondrous Cross**

# Speak for the Glory of God

*Day 19*

One of Africa's most interesting trees is the baobab tree. In a parched land, the baobab stands as a "Tree of Life," a blessing to those around it.[34] But the baobab is not your typical tree.[35] Its peculiar shape has a bloated, bulging trunk, a short, squatty crown, and branches that look like roots. For this reason, it's often called "the upside-down tree."[36]

Why is this tree so unique? The baobab is the world's largest succulent.[37] During the rainy season, it absorbs water like a giant sponge—expanding the trunk up to 36–46 feet in diameter![38]

Because of its unique design, the baobab is perfect for the African plains. It endures drought and produces some of the world's most nutritious fruit, known to treat diseases and strengthen immune systems.[39]

We live in a spiritually impoverished world, desperate for nutritious words. As God's ambassadors, we are called to stand like the baobab and feed life-giving words to hungry souls.

But is this easy? Not for me. Because of our sin nature, our tongues are a restless evil, full of deadly poison. The tongue may be small, but it wields great power. With it we bless, and with it we curse (James 3:1–12).

*So, what must we do?*

*How do we train our tongues?*

We must turn to the Lord and His Word.

Just as the baobab stores water in its trunk, we must store God's living water in our hearts (especially God's commands regarding our speech). When we do, nutritious words—words of wisdom, words of life—spring up so that we can be a means of grace to those who hear (Ephesians 4:29).

Is this your desire? It is mine! In this sin-cursed world, may His Word dwell richly within us (Colossians 3:16) so we can speak life-giving words for His glory and the blessing of others.

## Verses to Pray and Ponder

"The mouth of the righteous is a fountain of life."
**PROVERBS 10:11**

"The tongue of the wise brings healing."
**PROVERBS 12:18**

"A soft answer turns away wrath . . .
a gentle tongue is a tree of life."
**PROVERBS 15:1–4**

"To make an apt answer is a joy to a man,
a word in season, how good it is."
**PROVERBS 15:23**

"Gracious words are like a honeycomb,
sweetness to the soul and health to the body."
**PROVERBS 16:24**

"Let your speech always be gracious, seasoned with salt,
so that you may know how you ought to answer each person."
**COLOSSIANS 4:6**

"A word fitly spoken is like apples of gold in a setting of silver."
**PROVERBS 25:11**

## Prayer for the Day

*Lord,*
Set a guard over our mouths.
Bridle our tongues.
Make us quick to hear,
slow to speak.
Fill us with Your Holy Spirit.
Make our words God-breathed,
holy, and helpful,
full of grace and truth.
For Your glory alone,
*Amen.*

**Hymn for the Day: Make Me a Blessing**

# Work for the Glory of God

*Day 20*

Trees create, produce, and give to society. In other words, they have a job to do, a purpose to fulfill. For example:
- Oak trees provide lumber.
- Olive trees supply oil.
- Spruce trees yield paper.
- Maple trees produce syrup.

Like these trees, God created us for a special purpose. But, since we are created in His image, our work is sacred and superior. It's a holy calling with heavenly rewards.

Solomon explains in Ecclesiastes 3:10–13:

> I have seen the business that God has given to the children of man to be busy with…I perceived that there is nothing better for them than to be joyful and to do good as long as they live; also that everyone should eat and drink and take pleasure in all his toil—this is God's gift to man.

*What abilities has God given you?*

Sometimes, it can be hard to identify our unique talents, so pray and ask Him. Think about places where you like to serve and work. For example, if you like planning events, how can you use your planning skills elsewhere? Check with others if you're still unsure, as they may see your gifts and talents more clearly than you can.

Meanwhile, be faithful in the work God has assigned you today. Work heartily as an act of worship. He will lead you step-by-step.

Soon, our days will be over. While we can, let's work hard for that day when we will hear Him say, "Well done, good and faithful servant. You have been faithful over a little; I will set you over much. Enter into the joy of your master" (Matthew 25:21).

# Verses to Pray and Ponder

"Whatever your hand finds to do, do it with all your might."
**ECCLESIASTES 9:10**

"Go to the ant, O sluggard; consider her ways, and be wise.
Without having any chief, officer, or ruler,
she prepares her bread in summer and gathers her food in harvest."
**PROVERBS 6:6–8**

"The plans of the diligent lead surely to abundance."
**PROVERBS 21:5**

"Whatever you do, work heartily,
as for the Lord and not for men,
knowing that from the Lord you will receive the inheritance as your reward.
You are serving the Lord Christ."
**COLOSSIANS 3:23–24**

"Let the thief no longer steal, but rather let him labor,
doing honest work with his own hands,
so that he may have something to share with anyone in need."
**EPHESIANS 4:28**

## Prayer for the Day

*Lord,*
Thank You for the gift of work.
Lead us to the right vocation,
develop our skills,
and make us faithful in every season.
Give us wisdom, initiative, and creativity.
Deliver us from living a lazy life.
And help us to work hard,
serving You and blessing others
for Your glory alone.
In Your name,
*Amen.*

**Hymn for the Day: Living for Jesus**

# Sow Gospel Seeds

**Day 21**

Thump, thump, thump. There they go again! My oak trees are sowing seeds. Every year, scads of acorns drop to the ground.[40]

Oak trees are famous for their seeds. In a boom year, they can produce as many as 10,000, outshining all other nut-bearing trees.[41] These tiny treasures are a gift, packed with protein, to feed countless creatures.

Yet an even greater miracle occurs when one seed transforms into a tree. When conditions are right, the seed germinates, takes root, and emerges as a seedling. Over time, these seedlings grow into mighty oaks, and the cycle repeats itself.

God's blueprint for kingdom multiplication is almost identical. Just as God designed the oak tree to sow seeds, He designed us, His children, to sow spiritual seeds. We do this by sharing the gospel with neighbors, store clerks, coworkers, and anyone we meet. It's our primary calling as believers.

*What hinders you from sowing gospel seeds?*

*Do you lack concern for the lost?*

*Do you fear rejection?*

Studies show that oak trees fully exposed to sunlight produce more seeds. So, as God's servants, let's spend time in God's presence and soak up the warmth of His love through His Word. As we do, He will give us a heart for the lost and the boldness to share.

God is rescuing the perishing, with or without you. Will you join Him? Sowing seeds of faith is the greatest adventure on earth. The joy is unexplainable and unmatched by anything the world can offer. Don't miss it!

# Verses to Pray and Ponder

"And Jesus said to them,
'Follow me, and I will make you become fishers of men.'"
**Mark 1:17**

"For I am not ashamed of the gospel,
for it is the power of God for salvation to everyone who believes."
**Romans 1:16**

"But you will receive power when the Holy Spirit has come upon you,
and you will be my witnesses in Jerusalem and in all Judea and Samaria,
and to the end of the earth."
**Acts 1:8**

"Brothers, my heart's desire and prayer to God for them is that they may be saved."
**Romans 10:1**

"The harvest is plentiful, but the laborers are few.
Therefore pray earnestly to the Lord of the harvest
to send out laborers into his harvest."
**Luke 10:2**

"Go therefore and make disciples of all nations."
**Matthew 28:19**

## Prayer for the Day

*Father,*
Thank You for saving us.
As Your ambassadors,
give us the boldness to share this gift with others.
Open doors for us to sow gospel seeds
and spread Your fragrance everywhere we go.
In Jesus's name,
*Amen.*

**Hymn for the Day: Rescue the Perishing**

# Seek to Serve

*Day 22*

In contrast to the mighty oak and the soaring sequoias, the broom tree is short, unsightly, and sometimes scraggly. Yet for the weary traveler in ancient Israel, the broom tree was a welcome sight.[42] Underneath the prickly branches, weary souls found rest.[43]

The most notable example of a weary traveler is Elijah the prophet. Afraid and running for his life, Elijah sheltered under a broom tree. There in the shade of that spiny shrub, God strengthened him to continue his journey.

The Christian life is a marathon—long and exhausting. Even the strongest believers grow weary and want to quit. To run the race well, we need a broom tree experience along the way—someone to offer brief comfort, so we can continue our journey.

Jesus knew this better than anyone. He walked a weary road, yet as He suffered, He washed dirty feet, fed the hungry, and healed the sick. Jesus served (Mark 10:45) and commanded us to do the same.

*Are you weary of well-doing?*

*Does serving sound like a daunting task?*

Take heart! God sees and knows. He understands the sacrifice, and He will help you.

As the broom tree absorbs water through its deep roots, draw living water from God's Word. As you do, He will strengthen you so that you can help others.

Serving God is the pathway to a fruitful and fulfilling life. Serve for His glory, and the God who sees will remember and reward you for every good deed. (Matthew 10:42).

# Verses to Pray and Ponder

"The greatest among you shall be your servant."
**Matthew 23:11**

"Do not use your freedom as an opportunity for the flesh,
but through love serve one another."
**Galatians 5:13**

"Therefore, if anyone cleanses himself from what is dishonorable,
he will be a vessel for honorable use, set apart as holy,
useful to the master of the house, ready for every good work."
**2 Timothy 2:21**

"Do not be slothful in zeal, be fervent in spirit, serve the Lord."
**Romans 12:11**

"Bless, for to this you were called, that you may obtain a blessing."
**1 Peter 3:9**

"And let us not grow weary of doing good,
for in due season we will reap, if we do not give up.
So then, as we have opportunity, let us do good to everyone,
and especially to those who are of the household of faith."
**Galatians 6:9–10**

## Prayer for the Day

*Father,*
Help us lay down our lives and serve.
Make us clean vessels,
ready and willing to be used,
eager to hear Your voice
and follow Your lead.
In Your name,
we pray,
*Amen.*

**Hymn for the Day: Footsteps of Jesus**

# Use Your Spiritual Gifts

*Day 23*

In ancient times, date palms dotted the desert. Grand and glorious, they stood towering up to 100 feet high and bearing branches up to 20 feet long. In a barren land, God provided these trees at the right time and place to develop the ancient world.[44]

Every part of the date palm was useful. The trunks furnished building materials; the seeds produced oil; the dates curbed appetites; and the branches provided baskets, brooms, shade, and shelter. Nothing was wasted.[45]

Just as God created the date palm to bless the ancient world,[46] God created you to bless His kingdom (Ephesians 2:10). You are not a mistake. You are His treasure—handpicked, perfectly designed, and equipped with spiritual gifts to build His kingdom.

*Do you desire to use your gifts?*

Ask God to help you. Start by serving in your church. Join the cleaning crew, serve as a greeter, work in the nursery, teach a class. Be faithful in the little things, and He will lead you step-by-step. Over time, He will develop and energize your gifts for His glory and the spread of His kingdom.

You were born for such a time as this—this season, this place—for a purpose. Ask God to use you. He is eager to do so.

# Verses to Pray and Ponder

"For this reason I remind you to fan into flame the gift of God . . .
for God gave us a spirit not of fear but of power and love and self-control."
**2 Timothy 1:6–7**

"As each has received a gift, use it to serve one another,
as good stewards of God's varied grace:
whoever speaks, as one who speaks oracles of God;
whoever serves, as one who serves by the strength that God supplies
-in order that in everything God may be glorified through Jesus Christ."
**1 Peter 4:10–11**

"I say to everyone among you not to think of himself more highly
than he ought to think, but to think with sober judgment. . .
For as in one body we have many members,
and the members do not all have the same function. . .
Having gifts that differ according to the grace given to us,
let us use them: if prophecy, in proportion to our faith;
if service, in our serving; the one who teaches, in his teaching;
the one who exhorts, in his exhortation;
the one who contributes, in generosity;
the one who leads, with zeal;
the one who does acts of mercy, with cheerfulness."
**Romans 12:3-8**

## Prayer for the Day

*Father,*
Thank You.
You formed and fashioned us for a special purpose.
Help us to discover our gifts,
develop them,
and steward them well.
Equip us and empower us
to fulfill our callings.
May every day count for Your glory
and the advancement of Your kingdom.
In Your name,
*Amen.*

**Hymn for the Day: Take My Life and Let It Be Consecrated**

# PART V
## Weather the Storms

# Believe That God Is Sovereign

**Day 24**

Wildfires are devastating. Every year, the world loses millions of acres, hundreds of homes, and too many lives as fires ravage everything in their path.[47]

While many wildfires start from human error, some begin naturally from the right combination of heat, oxygen, and fuel. If coupled with fierce winds, a wildfire can spread rapidly and rage uncontrollably for days.

Afterward, the land appears hopeless. Yet amid the ashes stand the sequoias.[48] Fire is a friend to the sequoias, a blessing in disguise. It clears the underbrush, replenishes the soil, and causes sequoia cones to release thousands of seeds. When these seeds fall on prepared ground, baby sequoias sprout, and the forest multiplies.[49] Out of the ashes, God brings forth new life, trees that tower up to twenty-six stories high.[50]

In a fallen world, sin happens, and calamities come. Fiery trials can develop suddenly, threatening our lives and our homes. Many times, we are left in shock and deeply wounded.

But there is good news. Above the chaos, noise, and smoke, God is on His throne. He is sovereign. He not only controls fire, but He also controls the hearts of men and the circumstances surrounding our lives. Storms, disasters, fires, and floods are no surprise to Him.

So do not fear. Trials supply the perfect condition for God to showcase His grace and glory. He is our Redeemer, and for those who love Him, He works all things together for our good and for the blessing of others.

*Are you enduring a fiery trial (1 Peter 4:12)?*

*Do you feel like sin has left your life in ashes?*

Draw near to God. He sees and knows your pain. Jesus suffered deeper wounds, more devastating blows than we can imagine, so He understands. Trust Him. In time, He will bring beauty from ashes and tall trees from tiny seeds. To Him be the glory!

# Verses to Pray and Ponder

"The LORD has established His throne in the heavens,
and His sovereignty rules over all."
**PSALM 103:19 NASB**

"The king's heart is a stream of water in the hand of the LORD;
he turns it wherever he will."
**PROVERBS 21:1**

"The lot is cast into the lap, but its every decision is from the LORD."
**PROVERBS 16:33**

"The LORD said to him [Moses], 'Who has made man's mouth?
Who makes him mute, or deaf, or seeing, or blind?
Is it not I, the LORD.'"
**EXODUS 4:11**

"I am the LORD, and there is no other.
I form light and create darkness;
I make well-being and create calamity;
I am the LORD, who does all these things."
**ISAIAH 45:6–7**

"And we know that for those who love God all things work together for good,
for those who are called according to his purpose."
**ROMANS 8:28**

"For from him and through him and to him are all things.
To him be glory forever. Amen."
**ROMANS 11:36**

## Prayer for the Day

*Father,*
Thank You for these trials.
They hurt, but we trust You.
You are our rock and our refuge.
You control all things.
Redeem these ashes.
Weave these trials together for good.
Do amazing things and get great glory!
In Your name,
we pray,
*Amen.*

**Hymn for the Day: It Is Well with My Soul**

# Stand Firm in Your Faith

*Day 25*

When a hurricane approaches, people spring into action, stockpiling supplies, boarding windows, filling sandbags, gassing up cars, and fleeing to higher ground.

In contrast, the palm tree peacefully awaits the storm. Because of its flexible design, in high winds, the palm leaves fold in, and the wiry trunk begins to sway. The tree clings to its roots and braves the storm.

*How does the palm tree endure?*[51]

Unique from other tree roots, the palm tree forms a root ball, a solid anchor overlaid with hundreds of slender spaghetti-like roots. As long as the tree holds fast to its anchor, it can bend forty to fifty degrees and endure up to 145-mile-per-hour winds.[52]

Like hurricanes, personal storms interrupt our lives. But as Christians, we have nothing to fear. We are deeply rooted, forever fastened to Jesus Christ, our Rock. We may get whipped around; we may feel disheveled, but we will not be moved.

*Are the winds of affliction blowing in your face?*

*Are clouds gathering on the horizon?*

Run to Jesus. Spend time in His Word. Like the roots of a palm tree, cling to His promises. He will calm your fears and build your faith (Romans 10:17). You can trust Him.

# Verses to Pray and Ponder

"Do not be afraid of sudden terror nor of the ruin of the wicked,
when it comes, for the LORD will be your confidence."
**Proverbs 3:25–26**

"For we walk by faith, not by sight."
**2 Corinthians 5:7**

"For I, the LORD your God, hold your right hand; it is I who say to you,
'Fear not, I am the one who helps you.'"
**Isaiah 41:13**

"When you pass through the waters,
I will be with you; and through the rivers,
they shall not overwhelm you . . .
For I am the LORD your God . . .
your Savior."
**Isaiah 43:2–3**

"With man this is impossible, but with God all things are possible."
**Matthew 19:26**

"I know that you can do all things,
and that no purpose of yours can be thwarted."
**Job 42:2**

"Now to him who is able to do far more abundantly than all that we ask or think,
according to the power at work within us."
**Ephesians 3:20**

## Prayer for the Day

*Father,*
You control the storms of life.
Keep us rooted and grounded in Your Word.
Make us securely fastened to Your promises
so we can stand firm in our faith,
for Your glory,
and in Your name,
*Amen.*

**Hymn for the Day: The Solid Rock**

# Submit to God's Will

*Day 26*

Sitting on my back porch, I savored God's handiwork: the crystal blue sky, layers of green leaves, radiant red cardinals, and the sounds of woodpeckers. It was heavenly.

Yet, all was not perfect. A scampering squirrel leaped along a dead branch, reminding me the tree needed pruning.

Indeed, trees add beauty to our homes. But to flourish, they need pruning from time to time.[53] Without proper pruning, dead branches litter the landscape, making it ugly.[54]

*Like trees, we need pruning — spiritual pruning.*

Without it, we become proud and more of a problem to people than a blessing.

Thankfully, God, our arborist, loves us (Hebrews 12:6). So, with wisdom and skill, He trims away sin patterns. He smooths rough edges. He shapes us until we reflect His Son: perfect and complete, beautiful and bearing fruit (John 15:1–2).

While this process is painful, if we submit to His shears, He will create in us a humble heart and a life fit for service (Proverbs 3:11–12).

*Do you desire greater fruitfulness and usefulness?*

If so, submit to God (Luke 22:42). Ask Him to cut away anything contrary to His character. It sounds scary, but He is kind. His grace is sufficient (2 Corinthians 12:9). He will comfort you (2 Corinthians 1:3-5). And after a while, He will restore, confirm, strengthen, and establish you (1 Peter 5:10). It's worth it!

# Verses to Pray and Ponder

"Count it all joy, my brothers, when you meet trials of various kinds,
for you know that the testing of your faith produces steadfastness.
And let steadfastness have its full effect,
that you may be perfect and complete, lacking in nothing."
**JAMES 1:2-4**

"For the moment all discipline seems painful rather than pleasant,
but later it yields the peaceful fruit of righteousness
to those who have been trained by it."
**HEBREWS 12:11**

"'Shall we receive good from God, and shall we not receive evil?'
In all this Job did not sin with his lips."
**JOB 2:10**

"Thou he slay me, I will hope in him."
**JOB 13:15**

"Come, let us return to the LORD; for he has torn us,
that he may heal us;
he has struck us down, and he will bind us up."
**HOSEA 6:1**

"For I will restore health to you,
and your wounds I will heal,
declares the Lord.'"
**JEREMIAH 30:17**

## Prayer for the Day

*Father,*
Prune us,
shape us,
little by little,
day by day.
Make us like You.
Help us to humbly submit.
And please heal our wounds.
Remove any bitterness
so that we can bear much fruit,
in Your name
and for Your glory,
*Amen.*

**Hymn for the Day: Have Thine Own Way, Lord**

# Rejoice and Give Thanks

*Day 27*

Imagine trudging through a desert with the sun zapping your strength and sweat dripping from your brow. With no relief in sight, your heart sinks as you murmur, "Will this ever end?"

Sometimes, life can be like plodding through a desert. We easily grumble and complain. Yet, God commands us to "do all things without grumbling or disputing" (Philippians 2:14) and to "give thanks in all circumstances" (1 Thessalonians 5:18).

### *But, in the midst of trials, how is this possible?*

Apart from God, it's not. Let's learn from the Palo Verde tree.[55] In the American Southwest desert, Palo Verde trees flourish. God created them with green bark and deep roots, enabling them to thrive and bless a weary land. They provide oxygen, shelter for birds, food for wildlife, and flowers every spring.[56] What a beautiful example!

God desires His children to be a blessing—even in seasons of drought.

### *So what must we do?*

As the Palo Verde depends on its green trunk and deep roots to store water,[57] we must rely on God's Word (Psalm 119:92). It's a fountain of living water—a well that never runs dry. It's refreshing. As we drink, God strengthens us. He fills our hearts with joy (Nehemiah 8:10). And thanksgiving flows from our lips (Colossians 3:16).

### *What about you? Are you withering away in your circumstances?*

Drink deeply from God's Word and give thanks. He will make you a fragrant aroma and a bright light in this barren land.

# Verses to Pray and Ponder

"Give thanks in all circumstances;
for this is the will of God in Christ Jesus for you."
**1 Thessalonians 5:18**

"…The Lord gave, and the Lord has taken away;
blessed be the name of the Lord."
**Job 1:21**

"My mouth is filled with your praise,
and with your glory all the day."
**Psalm 71:8**

"Do all things without grumbling or disputing,
that you may be blameless and innocent,
children of God without blemish in the midst of a crooked and twisted generation,
among whom you shine as lights in the world."
**Philippians 2:14-15**

"Though the fig tree should not blossom, nor fruit be on the vines,
the produce of the olive fail and the fields yield no food,
the flock be cut off from the fold and there be no herd in the stalls,
yet I will rejoice in the LORD;
I will take joy in the God of my salvation."
**Habakkuk 3:17-18**

## Prayer for the Day

*Father,*
Forgive us for complaining.
Help us to give thanks in all things.
Cause our hearts to overflow with joy.
Open our lips to declare Your faithfulness.
Make us a fragrant aroma of Christ,
a bright light in this barren land,
for Your glory
and in Your name,
*Amen.*

**Hymn for the Day: Count Your Many Blessings**

# Pray Continually

Day 28

What is it about trees that calms our hearts and clears our minds?[58] Even the sight of their rich hues, textured bark, and lush leaves brings comfort and healing to our souls.

Trees exude peace and tranquility by their stillness. In a world of trouble, we yearn for that kind of peace.[59] God knows this and gives us a means to quiet our hearts and calm our fears: prayer (Philippians 4:6-7).

*Prayer soothes, sustains, and strengthens us to serve God.*

Look at the examples God has given us. Through prayer, Moses shepherded an obstinate nation. Daniel served a pagan king. David escaped relentless enemies. Paul endured imprisonment. Most importantly, Jesus carried our sorrows and was crushed for our iniquities (Isaiah 53:3, 5).

Jesus and these men had every reason to panic and succumb to fear, yet they prayed. In private prayer, they found peace and gathered strength to obey God, even in dire circumstances (Luke 22:41–44).

Just as prayer sustained Jesus and the saints of old, prayer will sustain you (Psalm 55:22).

*Are you weary?*

Run to Jesus, your strong tower (Proverbs 18:10). Find a room or a closet, get a chair, prepare a place, set a time, make a commitment. Cast your cares upon the Lord. And, He will turn your panic to peace, your fears to faith, and your weakness to strength. He will accomplish what concerns you, but you must pray.

# Verses to Pray and Ponder

"In the morning, O LORD, You will hear my voice;
In the morning I will order my prayer to You and eagerly watch."
**PSALM 5:3 NASB1995**

"When the righteous cry for help,
the LORD hears and delivers them out of all their troubles."
**PSALM 34:17**

"Pray without ceasing."
**1 THESSALONIANS 5:17**

"Ask, and it will be given to you; seek, and you will find;
knock, and it will be opened to you.
For everyone who asks receives, and the one who seeks finds,
and to the one who knocks it will be opened."
**MATTHEW 7:7–8**

"And this is the confidence that we have toward him,
that if we ask anything according to his will he hears us.
And if we know that he hears us in whatever we ask,
we know that we have the requests that we have asked of him."
**1 JOHN 5:14–15**

## Prayer for the Day

*Father,*
Forgive our anxious hearts.
Help us to lay our requests at Your feet
and leave them there.
Strengthen our weak arms and feeble knees.
Help us to persevere,
praying in the Spirit at all times.
May our prayers accomplish much for Your glory.
In Your name,
we pray,
*Amen.*

**Hymn for the Day: "I Must Tell Jesus**

# Fear God and Obey

*Day 29*

Only one tree symbolizes obedience—the cross of Christ. Historians are unsure what kind of tree the Romans used for crucifixion, but the exact type doesn't matter. What matters is that on a tree that God created, He crucified His only Son.

Like an innocent lamb going to the slaughter, Jesus obeyed His Father's command. In submission to His Father's will, He laid down, stretched out His arms, and allowed His enemies to pound nails into His hands and feet. He hung there, bled, and died.

Because Jesus is God, He could have commanded the angels to set Him free, but He didn't. He stayed the course, finished the race, and did His Father's will. The King of kings and the Lord of lords endured the most humiliating death known to man. Yet His obedience defeated the devil and purchased our pardon.

In this wicked world, God has paved a highway to heaven, the way of holiness (Isaiah 35:8). It's narrow, and it's hard. But do not fear. Jesus is seated at the right hand of God, and He will help you. He is interceding for you. He will give you grace and mercy to obey one day at a time, one step at a time (Hebrews 4:16).

### *Are you struggling to obey?*

Be careful!
- Never follow your flesh (1 John 2:15–17).
- Never trust your deceitful heart (Jeremiah 17:9).
- Never do what's right in your own eyes (Judges 17:6).

Instead, fix your eyes on Jesus, feed on His Word, and pray (Matthew 26:41). Surround yourself with believers and get accountability. He will empower you to obey.

Obedience is hard, but it's worth it. It accomplishes great things. God will be glorified, His kingdom will advance, and your descendants will be blessed. By His grace, let's be faithful unto death (Revelation 2:10). Reward is coming!

# Verses to Pray and Ponder

"Let everyone who names the name of the Lord depart from iniquity."
**2 Timothy 2:19**

"This blessing has fallen to me,
that I have kept your precepts."
**Psalm 119:56**

"I hasten and do not delay to keep your commandments."
**Psalm 119:60**

"Fear God and keep his commandments,
for this is the whole duty of man."
**Ecclesiastes 12:13**

"I delight to do your will, O my God;
your law is within my heart."
**Psalm 40:8**

"Let your eyes look directly forward,
and your gaze be straight before you.
Ponder the path of your feet;
then all your ways will be sure.
Do not swerve to the right or to the left;
turn your foot away from evil."
**Proverbs 4:25–27**

## Prayer for the Day

*Lord,*
Help us!
Plant our feet on the highway of holiness.
Help us to fear You.
Rescue us from every evil deed.
Keep us from stumbling.
Lord, have mercy.
Make us faithful to the end,
for Your glory
and in Your name,
*Amen.*

**Hymn for the Day: Trust and Obey**

# Be Still and Wait

*Day 30*

Every August, it's the same routine. I notice a lone leaf quietly floating to the ground. Fall is imminent. Fall is a spectacular season: blue sky, crisp air, and flaming trees. It's amazing, but it doesn't last long. Within a few weeks, crunchy leaves start piling up.

Soon, winter will transform beautiful branches into bare limbs.[60] It's a gloomy sight as the trees ease into a long winter's nap.[61]

Winter is a test of endurance. So, to survive, God designed trees to rest and rely on the food stored in their roots. The warm sunshine and lush leaves will return. But until then, they stand still and wait.

As Christians, we experience winter seasons as well—seasons of want and seasons of loss. It's God's design, and like deciduous trees, there is often nothing we can do except rest and wait on the Lord. But waiting is hard. Delayed desires make our hearts sick. Apart from God's Word, we succumb to discouragement and despair.

*Has God delayed your desires?*
*Are you weary of waiting?*

Be careful.
- Do not fear (Psalm 37:8).
- Do not quarrel with God (Isaiah 45:9–10).
- Do not try to force the desires of your heart (Genesis 16; Galatians 4:22–23).

Instead, rest and wait quietly. Leave the matter with God and do the next right thing. Seek Him, serve Him, love Him (1 Peter 1:8).

God is faithful. While we wait, He will work in an orderly and timely fashion. He will change hearts. He will weave circumstances together according to His pleasure. Just as spring will return, He will return with blessings (James 5:7–11). Rest assured, God fulfills His promises. He makes all things beautiful in His time (Ecclesiastes 3:11).

# Verses to Pray and Ponder

"Be still before the LORD and wait patiently for him."
**Psalm 37:7**

"The Lord will fight for you, while you keep silent."
**Exodus 14:14 NAS**

"Not by might, nor by power, but by my Spirit,
says the LORD of hosts."
**Zechariah 4:6**

"They who wait for the LORD shall renew their strength;
they shall mount up with wings like eagles;
they shall run and not be weary;
they shall walk and not faint."
**Isaiah 40:31**

"My soul waits for the Lord more than watchmen for the morning . . .
with the LORD there is steadfast love,
and with him is plentiful redemption.
And he will redeem Israel from all his iniquities."
**Psalm 130:6–8**

## Prayer for the Day

*Lord,*
Thank You for hearing our prayers.
While we wait, help us return to You and rest.
Help us trust Your timing and Your plan.
Help us dwell in the land and do good.
You will return with blessings.
You will act.
You will do great things.
To You be the glory,
*Amen.*

### Hymn for the Day: Have Faith in God

# Prepare for Heaven

*Day 31*

In the beginning, God placed Adam and Eve in the Garden of Eden. It was a lush sanctuary filled with plants and fruit trees, delicious to eat and delightful to the eyes. Amid the garden, God placed two special trees: the Tree of Life and the Tree of the Knowledge of Good and Evil. Adam and Eve were allowed to eat of the Tree of Life, but not of the Tree of Knowledge of Good and Evil. If they did, they would die.

The world was perfect until something horrible happened. Satan embodied a snake and deceived Adam and Eve. He lied and lured them to eat of the forbidden tree. At that moment, sin entered the world and altered the perfection of God's creation. As punishment, God banished Adam and Eve from the garden, sending them away from His presence and away from the Tree of Life.

As descendants of Adam and Eve, we inherited their corrupt nature. We were born enslaved to sin and likewise excluded from the presence of God and the Tree of Life. But thankfully, our story doesn't end there. Jesus Christ came to earth to pay the penalty for our sins. He died on a cross, and three days later, rose from the grave. Now, whoever believes in Him and repents of their sin is a new creation. God instantly restores our relationship with Him and makes us co-heirs with Christ (Romans 8:17).

*Are you carrying heavy burdens?*

Leave them in God's hands and look up! We are citizens of heaven! It's a joyful city, radiant like the sun, filled with the glory of God. The foundation sparkles with jewels. The streets gleam with gold. The walls are jasper. The gates are pearls. And beside the crystal river stands the Tree of Life, bearing fresh fruit and life-giving leaves (Revelation 22:1–5).

In God's celestial city, we will see Him face to face. He will richly reward us and make up for our sufferings (2 Corinthians 4:17–18). This is our inheritance. This is our home. Do you long for that day? I do! Until then, let's run the race. Let's get ready. Because soon, He will take us home. And, oh, what a day that will be when we see His face and hear Him say: "Well done, good and faithful servant . . . Enter into the joy of your master" (Matthew 25:21).

# Verses to Pray and Ponder

"Jesus said . . . 'No one who puts his hand to the plow
and looks back is fit for the kingdom of God.'"
**Luke 9:62**

"But one thing I do: forgetting what lies behind and straining forward to
what lies ahead,
I press on toward the goal for the prize of the upward call of God in Christ Jesus."
**Philippians 3:13–14**

"Let us also lay aside every weight, and sin which clings so closely,
and let us run with endurance the race that is set before us."
**Hebrews 12:1**

"Seek the things that are above, where Christ is, seated at the right hand of God."
**Colossians 3:1**

"Do not lay up for yourselves treasures on earth,
where moth and rust destroy and where thieves break in and steal,
but lay up for yourselves treasures in heaven,
where neither moth nor rust destroys and where thieves do not break in and steal.
For where your treasure is, there your heart will be also."
**Matthew 6:19–21**

"My soul longs, yes, faints for the courts of the LORD. . .
For a day in your courts is better than a thousand elsewhere."
**Psalm 84:2, 10**

## Prayer for the Day

*Lord,*
Thank You.
You have blessed us beyond measure:
a heavenly home, a crown,
an inheritance.
Help us to fix our eyes on You
and the joy set before us.
Help us to prepare for and yearn for that perfect city,
filled with Your glory
and the riches of Your grace.
In Jesus's name,
*Amen.*

**Hymn for the Day: When We All Get to Heaven**

# Conclusion

What season of life are you in? Older, younger, middle-aged? Maybe you're enjoying a season of blessing. Or perhaps you feel stuck in a deep valley.

Whatever the season, give thanks. God is at hand. He will help you. Even in this weary world, He can transform you into a life-giving tree.

So, let's seek the Lord.
Let's read His Word and pray.
He will answer.
In His time, He will make us like a forest of living trees!

## Closing Prayer

*Lord,*
Thank You for saving us and for Your Word.
Help us to treasure Scripture above all things.
Help us to walk in the Spirit and make us a blessing.
Make us life-givers who produce much fruit for Your glory.
And cause Your gospel to spread across the globe.
In Your name,
we pray,
*Amen.*

# Money Verses

Money is a gift from the Lord, but it can also be a thorn (Matthew 13:7, 22). It can derail us from loving God and bearing fruit. So, take these verses seriously. Memorize them. Dig through the Word and find more. God has a lot to say about money, so let's learn all we can. Money is not our friend. It's a resource to be used for His glory.

"Honor the Lord with your wealth and with the first fruits of all your produce; then your barns will be filled with plenty, and your vats will be bursting with wine."
**Proverbs 3:9–10**

"Whoever has a bountiful eye will be blessed, for he shares his bread with the poor."
**Proverbs 22:9**

"It is well with the man who deals generously and lends; who conducts his affairs with justice."
**Psalm 112:5**

"Do not toil to acquire wealth; be discerning enough to desist. When your eyes light on it, it is gone, for suddenly it sprouts wings, flying like an eagle toward heaven."
**Proverbs 23:4–5**

"No one can serve two masters, for either he will hate the one and love the other, or he will be devoted to the one and despise the other. You cannot serve God and money."
**Matthew 6:24**

"For the love of money is a root of all kinds of evils.
It is through this craving that some have wandered away from the faith
and pierced themselves with many pangs."
1 T??????? 6:10

"Keep your life free from love of money, and be content with what you have,
for he has said, 'I will never leave you nor forsake you.'"
H??????? 13:5

## Prayer

L???,

You are Jehovah Jireh,
our Provider.
Remove greed from our hearts
and make us faithful with every penny.
Give us grace to use the money we earn for Your glory,
the spread of Your kingdom,
and the blessing of others.
In Jesus's name,
A???.

## Hymn: I'd Rather Have Jesus

# Action Points

Below are practical ways to apply some of the truths in this devotional. Make it a point to do at least one per month. Consider asking a friend to join you and keep you accountable.

1. Serve someone without anyone else knowing about it. Bring a meal, send an encouraging note, leave flowers on someone's doorstep, and see where God leads you.
2. Put a Scripture verse on your screensaver.
3. Illustrate a Scripture verse with colored pencils or some other creative way.
4. Is there something polluting your mind? What are you watching that is unhealthy? Put it away.
5. In every situation, ask, "How can I serve? How can I bless others?"
6. While driving to church on Sunday, ask God to use you to love and encourage others. Speak God's Words and be His hands and feet.
7. Ask God to open a door to share the gospel. Keep tracts in your purse, in your car, or at your front door to give to the delivery driver.
8. Get an accountability partner to confess that stubborn sin you can't seem to get rid of.
9. Instead of wasting time on the internet or on irrelevant things, encourage someone, learn a new skill, or read a good book.
10. Read through Proverbs, one chapter per day. Highlight in yellow all the speech verses. The following month, highlight in green all the money verses.
11. Read and/or sing at least one hymn every morning.
12. Daily, thank God for everything. Start small: your shoes, clothes, hair, trees, grass, sky, even the air you breathe. The list never ends. And you will find joy.
13. Keep a prayer journal. Write down your worries each morning. Cast them upon the Lord and watch Him work.
14. Ask God to help you love your enemies or those who have hurt you (Matthew 5:43–48). Think of tangible ways to show them love; pray for them.
15. Memorize Scripture verses. Put them on your bathroom mirror, in your car, above your kitchen sink. Meditate on them, and they will trickle from your head to your heart. Scripture hidden in our hearts keeps us from sin (Psalm 119:11).

# Additional Hymns

I grew up with hymns that were rich in theology. I love them, so choosing only one hymn for each day was agonizing. To relieve my pain, I decided to add this appendix with additional hymns. I encourage you to study the lyrics and sing/say them to the Lord. They will strengthen you and help you overcome whatever it is you are facing.

Heaven Came Down
At Calvary
The Old Rugged Cross
At the Cross
Only Trust Him
Jesus Paid It All
He Lives
I Need Thee Every Hour
Leaning on the Everlasting Arms
My Savior's Love
Man of Sorrows! What a Name
Holy, Holy, Holy! Lord God Almighty
Turn Your Eyes Upon Jesus
There Is a Fountain
Are You Washed in the Blood
Grace Greater Than Our Sin
Wonderful Grace of Jesus
He Hideth My Soul
Tell Me the Old, Old Story
I Am Thine, O Lord
Come Thou Fount of Every Blessing
All That Thrills My Soul
Jesus Is All the World to Me
Revive Us Again
How Great Thou Art
Rock of Ages
Send the Light
I Love to Tell the Story

We've A Story to Tell to the Nations
Song for the Nations
Bringing in the Sheaves
His Eye is on the Sparrow
Crown Him with Many Crowns
I Will Sing of My Redeemer
'Tis So Sweet to Trust in Jesus
Standing on the Promises
Higher Ground
My Faith Has Found a Resting Place
My Faith Looks Up to Thee
He Keeps Me Singing
Redeemed, How I Love to Proclaim It!
All Creatures of Our God and King
To God Be the Glory
What a Friend We Have in Jesus
In the Garden
Sweet Hour of Prayer
Savior, like a Shepherd Lead Us
The Way of the Cross Leads Home
He Leadeth Me
There Shall Be Showers of Blessing
Near to the Heart of God
Great Is Thy Faithfulness
On Jordan's Stormy Banks
I'll Fly Away
When the Roll is Called Up Yonder
We're Marching to Zion
Blessed Assurance

# Acknowledgments

Thank you to Rod, my husband, who supported me and loved me while I sat at the kitchen table hour after hour working on this project. You are far more than I deserve.

Thank you to Grace Church of Gainesville, a beautiful forest of life-giving trees. I am blessed to serve and live among you.

Thank you to Jenny Williams, Heather Judkins, Cheryl Warner, Christy Garcia, and Andrea Felts who generously helped with bits and pieces.

Thank you to Amber Joyce, who sacrificially edited the manuscript in its earlier stages. I know it was painful to read, as it was loaded with too much information.

Thank you to the advisors and editors who helped along the way: Laura Allnut, Debbie Wilson, Sarah Hamaker, and Melanie Chitwood. Your contributions were invaluable.

Thank you to April Pierce, Wendy Ricketts, and Denise Ball, who read the final draft and provided necessary, on-point feedback.

Thank you to the staff at Lucid Books. Even though I knew nothing about publishing, you were patient and easy to work with.

Finally, thank you to *my Lord and Savior, Jesus Christ.* Without You, I am nothing. I love You so much.

# About the Author

APRIL FULTZ was born and raised in West Texas; she came to know Jesus personally while living in Lubbock, Texas. While attending Southwestern Seminary, she met Rod, the man she would marry, and together they served in missions work in Africa, Texas, and Florida. In 2001, God led them to plant Grace Church in Gainesville, Virginia, where Rod has served as senior pastor ever since. God has blessed them with four amazing adult children, three daughters-in-law, five grandchildren, and a loving church family.

# Notes

1. Susan Hunt, *The True Woman: The Beauty & Strength of a Godly Woman* (Crossway, 2019).
2. "Why Do Some Years Produce More Acorns Than Others?" Mass Audubon, October 13, 2023, https://blogs.massaudubon.org/yourgreatoutdoors/about-those-acorns/.
3. "The Endicott Pear Tree, Still Alive in Massachusetts after Nearly 400 Years," New England Historical Society, accessed May 8, 2024, https://www.newenglandhistoricalsociety.com/endicott-pear-tree-still-alive-massachusetts-nearly-400-years/.
4. Richard B. Trask, "What a Pear: A Brief History of the Endecott Pear Tree," Danvers Archival Center at the Peabody Institute Library, https://www.danverslibrary.org/archive/what-a-pear/.
5. "Tree Roots," Cherokee Tree Care, June 23, 2023. https://www.cherokeetreecare.com/tree-roots.
6. Mary Simpson, "The Root System of Oak Trees," Week&, last updated December 14, 2018, https://www.weekand.com/home-garden/article/root-system-oak-trees-18023400.php.
7. TreeNewal Staff, "The Root System of Oak Trees: The Essential Guide," TreeNewal (blog), May 3, 2022, https://treenewal.com/the-root-system-of-oak-trees-the-essential-guide/.
8. Elizabeth Durham, "Weeping Willow Facts: 9 Common Questions, Answered," FastGrowingTrees, last updated June 16, 2022, https://www.fast-growing-trees.com/pages/weeping-willow-facts-9-common-questions-answered.
9. Viveka Neveln, "How To Plant And Grow Weeping Willow," Better Homes & Gardens, last updated April 18, 2024, https://www.bhg.com/gardening/plant-dictionary/tree/weeping-willow
10. Sarah Moore, "What Is Fungus on a Tree & Can It Affect Anyone?" Week&, last updated November 11, 2019, https://www.weekand.com/home-garden/article/fungus-tree-can-affect-anyone-18048823.php.
11. Tyler Lacoma, "How to Identify (and Treat) Common Tree Fungus Species," Angi, last updated January 16, 2024, https://www.angi.com/articles/3-common-tree-diseases.htm.
12. "My Tree Has a Lean, What Does That Mean?" TreesCharlotte, May 26, 2021, https://treescharlotte.org/tree-education/my-tree-has-a-lean-what-does-that-mean/.
13. "Leaning Towards the Light," The Climb by Dene E. Gainey, https://denegainey.com/dene-gainey/2020/5/23/leaning-towards-the-light.
14. Cameron Duncan, "Acacias V Giraffes – A Uniquely African Tussle," African Safari Consultants, November 4, 2011, https://www.africansafaris.com/acacias-v-giraffes-a-uniquely-african-tussle/.
15. Eyder Peralta, "Man Accused of Poisoning Toomer's Corner Oaks Apologizes to Auburn," NPR, September 29, 2011, https://www.npr.org/sections/thetwo-way/2011/09/29/140934596/man-accused-of-poisoning-toomers-corner-oaks-apologizes-to-auburn.
16. Auburn Traditions | Rolling Toomer's Corner," Auburn Tigers Official Athletics Website, https://auburntigers.com/traditions-rolling-toomers-corner.
17. Andrea Thompson, "Meet the Giant Sequoia, the 'Super Tree' Built to Withstand Fire," Scientific American, July 15, 2022, https://www.scientificamerican.com/article/meet-the-giant-sequoia-the-super-tree-built-to-withstand-fire/.
18. Tom Hennigan, "Talking Trees—Secrets of Plant Communication," Answers in Genesis, accessed May 8, 2024, https://answersingenesis.org/biology/plants/talking-trees/.

19  Rion Nakaya, "The Wood Wide Web: How Trees Secretly Talk to and Share with Each Other," The Kid Should See This, October 5, 2023, https://thekidshouldseethis.com/post/the-wood-wide-web-how-trees-secretly-talk-to-and-share-with-each-other.

20  "How to Kill and Get Rid of Formosan Termites" PestSupply, https://www.epestsupply.com/formosan_termites.php#.X4BKHC9h2S4.

21  Jonathan Tyler Quinn Farkas, "How to Get Rid of Formosan Termites," Today's Homeowner with Danny Lipford, last updated September 25, 2024, https://todayshomeowner.com/pest-control/guides/formosan-termites-a-growing-threat/.

22  Raven Wisdom, "Everything You Need to Know about Tumbleweeds," LawnStarter, October 30, 2023, https://www.lawnstarter.com/blog/lawn-care-2/everything-you-need-to-know-about-tumbleweeds

23  "Russian thistle," Methow Conservancy, https://methowconservancy.org/weeds/russian-thistle.

24  "Tumbleweed," DesertUSA, accessed June 23, 2023 https://www.desertusa.com/flowers/tumbleweed.html.

25  Emily Osterloff, "Tumbleweeds: The Fastest Plant Invasion in the USA's History," Natural History Museum, https://www.nhm.ac.uk/discover/tumbleweeds-fastest-plant-invasion-in-usa-history.html.

26  "Dealing with Tree Suckers," Love Your Landscape.ORG, https://www.loveyourlandscape.org/expert-advice/tree-care/insects-and-disease/dealing-with-tree-suckers/.

27  Heather Rhoades, "Tree Sucker Removal and Tree Sucker Control," gardeningknowhow, last updated June 21, 2021, https://www.gardeningknowhow.com/ornamental/trees/tgen/tree-sucker-removal-and-tree-sucker-control.htm.

28  Joanna Mounce Stancil, The Power of One Tree – The Very Air We Breathe," U.S. Department of Agriculture, March 17, 2015, https://www.usda.gov/media/blog/2015/03/17/power-one-tree-very-air-we-breathe.

29  "Tree Facts," Arbor Day Foundation, https://www.arborday.org/trees/treefacts/.

30  "The Love Trees of St. Augustine," Atlas Obscura, August 19, 2012, https://www.atlasobscura.com/places/the-love-trees-of-st-augustine-st-augustine-florida.

31  Angela Nelson, "What is Crown Shyness?" Treehugger, last updated May 2, 2019, https://www.treehugger.com/what-is-crown-shyness-4869713.

32  James MacDonald, "The Mysteries of Crown Shyness," JSTOR Daily, August 25, 2018, https://daily.jstor.org/the-mysteries-of-crown-shyness/.

33  Andrew Murray, Humility, Harold J. Chadwick, ed. (Bridge Logos Foundation, 2001).

34  Maryann Readal, "Baobab Tree – the African 'Tree of life,'" The Herb Society of America (blog), September 19, 2022, https://herbsocietyblog.wordpress.com/2022/09/19/baobab-tree-the-african-tree-of-life/.

35  "Fun Facts about the Baobab Tree," SecretAfrica, August 30, 2019, https://secretafrica.com/fun-facts-about-the-baobab-tree/.

36  Megan Ware, "Health and Nutritional Benefits of Boabab," Medical News Today, February 27, 2018, https://www.medicalnewstoday.com/articles/306445#benefits.

37  "Adansonia digitata (African Baobab)," World of Succulents, https://worldofsucculents.com/adansonia-digitata/.

38  "Mystery of the Weird and Wonderful 'Upside-Down Tree'" Finally Solved," Discover Wildlife, https://www.discoverwildlife.com/plant-facts/trees/mystery-of-wandering-upside-down-tree-finally-solved.

39  Geeta Maker-Clark, Is Africa's Ancient Baobab Tree Growing the Next Superfood?" National Geographic, May 1, 2016, https://www.nationalgeographic.com/culture/article/is-baobab-africas-ancient-tree-of-life-the-next-superfruit.

40  TreeNewal Staff, "Acorns and Oak Trees: Everything You Need to Know," May 16, 2022, https://treenewal.com/acorns-and-oak-trees-everything-you-need-to-know

41    "Why Are There So Many Acorns This Year? Do They Predict a Harsh Winter?" Plant and Gardening FAQ, NYBG Mertz Library Reference, last updated March 18, 2024, https://libanswers.nybg.org/faq/222824.

42    Bob Dodson, "Shade: Biblical Imagery & the Broom Tree, Acts 242 Study, February 18, 2009, https://acts242study.com/shade-biblical-imagery-the-broom-tree/.

43    Bob Dodson, "Shade: Biblical Imagery & the Broom Tree, Acts 242 Study, February 18, 2009, https://acts242study.com/shade-biblical-imagery-the-broom-tree/.

44    Wikipedia, "Date Palm," last modified August 18, 2024, https://en.wikipedia.org/wiki/Date_palm.

45    ChihCheng T. Chao and Robert R. Krueger, "The Date Palm (Phoenix dactylifera L.): Overview of Biology, Uses, and Cultivation," HortScience, 42, no.5 (2007): 1077–1082, https://journals.ashs.org/hortsci/view/journals/hortsci/42/5/article-p1077.xml#d958986e218.

46    "Ancient Bible References to Date Palm Phoenix dactylifera," The Nursery at TyTy, https://www.tytyga.com/Ancient-Bible-References-to-Date-Palm-Trees-Phoenix-dactylifera-a/328.htm.

47    "Wildland Fire Facts: There Must Be All Three," National Park Service, last updated October 19, 2023, https://www.nps.gov/articles/wildlandfire-facts-fuel-heat-oxygen.htm

48    Ezra D. Romero, "After Rough Fire, Millions of Giant Sequoia Seedlings Take Root," KQED Valley Public Radio, May 14, 2016, https://www.kqed.org/news/10953916/months-after-rough-fire-millions-of-giant-sequoia-seedlings-take-root.

49    Brian Clark Howard, "How Sequoias Survive Wildfires, in Yosemite and Beyond," National Geographic, August 26, 2023, https://www.nationalgeographic.com/science/article/130826-giant-sequoias-yosemite-rim-fire-forestry-science.

50    "The Largest Trees in the World," National Park Service, last updated November 23, 2023, https://www.nps.gov/seki/learn/nature/largest-trees-in-world.htm.

51    Melissa Breyer, "How Do Palm Trees Survive Hurricanes?" Treehugger, last updated October 9, 2020, https://www.treehugger.com/how-do-palm-trees-survive-hurricanes-4858412.

52    Caitlin Olson, "How Do Palm Trees Survive Hurricane Winds?" Today You Should Know, March 21, 2024, https://www.todayyoushouldknow.com/articles/how-do-palm-trees-survive-hurricane-winds.

53    Chris McLaughlan, "10 Reasons Why You Should Prune Trees & Shrubs," BBB Seed, July 5, 2021, Wildflower Seeds. https://bbbseed.com/10-reasons-why-you-should-prune-trees-and-shrubs/.

54    "How Trees Recover from Wounds and Pruning," May 15, 2019, https://medium.com/@FastTreeRemovalServices-Atlanta/how-trees-recover-wounds-pruning-18e1926872b5.

55    "Iconic Desert Tree: The Palo Verde," AZPlant Lady, https://www.azplantlady.com/2009/09/iconic-desert-tree-palo-verde.html.

56    Melissa Pino "Palo Verde Tree: Description, Types, Facts, and Care Tips," Planet Natural Research Center, last updated September 9, 2024, https://www.planetnatural.com/palo-verde-tree

57    "Palo Verde Tree," Arizona State Parks & Trails, https://azstateparks.com/palo-verde-tree

58    Alex Hutchinson, "How Trees Calm Us Down," The New Yorker, July 23,205, https://www.newyorker.com/tech/annals-of-technology/what-is-a-tree-worth.

59    Richard E. Cytowic, "Stressed Out? Science Says Look at Some Trees," Psychology Today, May 16, 2016, https://www.psychologytoday.com/us/blog/the-fallible-mind/201605/stressed-out-science-says-look-some-trees.

60    Andrew Moore, "How Trees Survive in Winter," NC State University College of Natural Resources News, February 15, 2024, https://cnr.ncsu.edu/news/2024/02/how-trees-survive-in-winter.

61    Rebecca Reynandez, "How Trees Survive Cold Winters," Project Learning Tree, https://www.plt.org/educator-tips/how-trees-survive-cold-winters/.

www.ingramcontent.com/pod-product-compliance
Lightning Source LLC
Chambersburg PA
CBHW060925170426
43192CB00024B/2894